Preface

It was a cool crisp Sept
military interested me.
counter staring, switching back and forth between my half
eaten Hot Pocket and our kitchen television set which displayed
the image of two large sky scrapers ablaze in New York City. I
remember thinking to myself, "How could the pilots of those
planes not see the buildings that they just crashed into?" As the
story developed and I got ready for my day at school, my
mother explained to me that those planes had bad people in
them and flew the planes into the towers on purpose. As a third
grader, I finally made the realization that America had enemies.

Earlier that year Pearl Harbor, starring Ben Affleck had hit the
big screen. I remember going to see it in the theaters with my
Dad. I was enthralled with every aspect of the military from that
point on. The structure, the leadership style, the comradery,
and even though I was young, all the girls the soldiers in the
movie got. For the next several months, playing with my
neighborhood friends I would imagine myself as a pilot shooting
down Japanese Zeros and rescuing POWs from Japanese prison
camps. Whenever, I was shot down by one of my buddies (this
was a rare occasion because I made the rules of the game) I
would eject myself out of the plane, land safely on the ground,
and find a way to get my revenge. I have fond memories of
dashing under enemy fire, breeching doors, filling rooms full of
hot lead, and rescuing those in distress. At age nine I was
already a bona fide Rambo and a proud owner of nearly every
WWII era G.I. Joe on the market.

Fast forward to my kitchen counter I slowly began to make the
connection between the Japanese attack on Pearl Harbor during

WWII and the terrorist attacks that took place on September 11, 2001. However, unlike the actors in Pearl Harbor, real people lost their lives in those towers, at the Pentagon, and in that field in Pennsylvania. After watching countless rescues from Ground Zero, it became apparent to me that there were no glorified heroes on September 11th, just Americans fulfilling their civil duties, putting the well-being of others before themselves, and contributing to what makes this country great. Even though it was such a tragic day, I was filled with a great sense of pride for my country. I was proud of our nation, proud of those who died and those who risked their lives to help others. I had the sudden realization that my country had done many things for me, yet besides saying the Pledge of Allegiance every day, I had done nothing for it. I realized that America had allowed me to go to school, play with my friends, stay out late, and eat pancakes for dinner; but what had I done? From this day forward I knew that I was in debt to my country and I knew just the way to pay it back.

Chapter 1

High School

17, 18, 18, 19, 21. Those were the scores I received on my ACT exam, a comprehensive standardized test out of 36 possible points that is supposed to be an indicator of how well any given student will perform at the college level. With scores this low I would consider myself lucky if I was accepted into any other school besides my local state university. After my fourth attempt at this test I was pretty much ready to kiss my pending academic scholarship to Occidental University to play Division III football and my Congressional appointment to the United States Merchant Marine Academy goodbye forever. I blame my public school education. At a whopping 215lbs with average strength, below average speed, and only a second team All-District recognition I was no prospect for any junior college football team and God knows there was no way I was about to try and walk on to the team at State. By this time it was February of 2009, spring semester of my senior year in high school and I had no idea what I would be doing upon graduation. This lack of security frustrated my mother and step-father more so than me. I knew I needed to make plans for my future but I was more worried about drinking beer, tailgating at the local Sonic Drive-In, and trying to find a Prom date (which I did).

I can't say I completely ignored my plans for the future. Even though it had been covered up with football, parties on the weekends, and petty part-time jobs I still had a burning desire to serve my country in some fashion. I had been in contact with Staff Sergeant (SSG) Tellez, a local Marine recruiter who had somehow gotten my phone number. Speaking with SSG Tellez one Saturday afternoon re-ignited my desire to serve in the military. After my meeting with SSG Tellez I went on to share my re-found obligatory feelings of service to my parents who then decided to take it upon themselves to further investigate my interest in the military. My mother was hesitant at first, but she knew the military had great things to offer young adults.

After a long day at the pawn shop, where I worked, my mother approached me with an idea that would change my life forever. "Reserve Officer Training Corps" she said. I replied back with, "You mean those nerds (I actually used to be one early on in high school) who march around on the basketball courts in those starchy uniforms? No way, I tried that before, yeah some of it was cool but everyone was just so lame." From the look she sent firing back at me I knew this had been a find she thought for sure I would be excited about. I gulped hard and decided to listen to what she had to say. She had me watch a couple of videos that got me a little bit excited and then I remembered that one of my best friends and teammate's Dad was an Army ROTC instructor at New Mexico State University. However, by this time my mom was way ahead of me and had already invited my friend's entire family over for dinner to discuss Army ROTC later that week. My mom was and still is today always organizing meetings for me with professionals in career fields that I am interested in. I always thought they were pointless but now I couldn't be more grateful that she took the time to do this for me. Thanks Mom.

During that dinner I learned that through the Federal Army ROTC Scholarship, if selected, I would receive fully paid tuition and fees to any institution that had or was aligned with an Army ROTC Program that I could get accepted to. After hearing this I was so excited, sorting through all the different places I ever wanted to live that I almost didn't hear him say that upon graduation I would owe a total of eight years back to the Army as an officer(Four years Active Duty and Four years Reserve Duty). Major Nakamoto was very deliberate and careful the way he spoke about the program. He was speaking to me with an almost father-like tone. By no means was he trying to recruit me. In fact, after dinner he pulled me aside and asked me if it was me or my parents that were more interested in the military. He told me that often parents are so attracted by the fact that the ROTC route is a way to get their child's full college education paid for that they end up forcing the decision upon the child. He said that he had seen this happen way too many times and the end result was never good. Additionally, he conveyed to me that even though he had had a successful Army career and been able to create a good life for his wife and kids that he would never want any of his children in today's military. I thought this was odd coming from a guy with 20 plus years of service. When I asked him why he felt this way he conveyed to me the expendability of soldiers and officers in the Army. "When you enter into the military" he said, "you immediately give up every ounce of individualism you have inside of you." Being a person who had played team sports my entire life, I thought I knew exactly what he was talking about. Boy was I wrong. "You think anyone in the Army gives a damn about whether you live or die?" he blurted while he dug is finger into my chest. "You are expendable, that's what makes our Army the best in the world. We can replace you in a matter of seconds and no one will know the difference." He looked down, "The mother of every service member gets the same folded flag at her son or daughters funeral, and that's the end of it." As I stood there on my back patio, stunned at what I had just heard, I listened to him go on to tell me that he thought my attitude toward serving my country was admirable, but he wanted me to think long and hard about the current conflicts that were occurring in Iraq and Afghanistan and all the people I would leave behind if I were gone.

That night put a lot of things in perspective for me. I knew I would have a lot of thinking and praying to do about serving in the military. Not fully knowing what I wanted to do, my mom thought it best to go forth and apply for the scholarship while I continued to explore other options just in case.

As time went on and I halfheartedly Google searched ways to pay for college, several past experiences kept popping into my mind. I consistently reminded myself of the events that took place on September 11th and how I felt in debt to my country. Pearl Harbor remained to be one of my favorite movies and every time I watched it I was more and more intrigued by its mere power and demonstration of patriotism. Additionally, since football season was over and my only other activity other than school was working at the pawn shop, I didn't know it at the time, but I missed not being part of a team. I missed working hard and giving my all with a group of people I had come to love, working towards a common goal, doing whatever it took to be successful. I desperately needed to be part of something bigger than myself. After finally realizing this, I was notified that I had been selected for a four-year Federal Army ROTC Scholarship.

Lessons learned:

1. Don't just go with the flow. Sometimes to get what you want you have to step outside of your comfort zone.
2. They say children are truthful and will always say what's on their mind. Find your inner child and follow your

early childhood ambitions, fore you know they are genuine.

3. Networking is Key. Find a person who has excelled in your area of interest, pick that person's brain, and allow that person to mentor you through the process.

Chapter 2

Awards

I had to get off work early that day because I had to go to the "Mandatory" Senior Awards presentation that evening at the high school. I pulled into the parking lot and walked into the lobby of the gym where all the seniors were supposed to meet and change into our cap and gowns. Thanks to my time playing football it had become my nature to show up to everything fifteen minutes early (little did I know this would become one of the single most important things I ever learned). I was the only one in the lobby. Finally, everyone began to show up and the ceremony began. I was not expecting to get any awards or be recognized for anything so I was a little confused as to why my parents had made such a big deal about any of us attending. The awards were first, valedictorian, salutatorian, top English student, top math student, blah blah blah. I was more worried about what I was going to have for dinner.

Then the principal went to the podium and began reading off the different scholarships that some of the students had been awarded. I zoned out during this little presentation too. Then I noticed something, or someone rather standing behind the stage. A tall man in an a very decorative all green uniform holding a very large cardboard check, similar to the ones you see on TV game shows or at golf tournaments. It was a matter of seconds before the principal introduced this man to the crowd as," Staff Sergeant Jameson, who has a very special award to present tonight." As the man approached the podium I sat up in my seat and he began to speak. I have no idea what he said because the next thing I knew the crowd had erupted into applause and all my football buddies sitting next to me were slapping me on the back and messing up my cap and tassel. As I made my way to the podium, I was so confused. Before I made my way up the stairs on to the stage I unsuccessfully tried to locate my mom in the crowd, hoping she could shoot me a sign of confidence to numb my nerves. I walked up to the man, shook his hand with one hand, grasped the check with the other, and made some kind of motion with my mouth that almost resembled a smile and accepted my Four Year Federal Army ROTC Scholarship. Guess it was a good thing that I showed up to this event after all.

As I made my way back to my seat, again I searched for my mom in the crowd, finally spotting her. When we made eye contact, with tears in her eyes she smiled and immediately the shakiness that had penetrated my legs disappeared and my whole body was inflated with pride. I sat back down proud to be her son and proud to be an American. I was ready to serve.

Lessons learned:

1. Show up to events where people are being recognized. You never know, you may just find yourself up on stage holding a big check.

Chapter 3

Almost outta here

As graduation neared the college acceptance and rejection letters began to fill our mailbox. However, I didn't take the time to apply that many places so I guess the mailbox wasn't that full. After being accepted and visiting the campus and ROTC program at The University of Arizona I decided I would apply my Federal Army ROTC Scholarship to there. Both sides of my family have a history at the UA, as it is called. My mom, aunt, two of my uncles, and three of my cousins all attended the UA. When I told each of them that I would be attending the UA all of them were overjoyed! However, to my mom's fear they all told me all of their uncensored accounts of college life in Tucson. I knew I this would be one wild ride.

I spent the entire summer working out and watching what I ate in preparation for the dreaded Army Physical Fitness Test that I had to pass in order to be awarded my scholarship. The Army Physical Fitness Test or APFT is a comprehensive fitness exam that tests an individual's strength and endurance through a two minute timed interval of push-ups and sit-ups followed by a two-mile run. As a lineman in high school, I was not one for endurance events or eating healthy. However, I was motivated and knew that just like those individuals who died serving their country on September 11th I would have to make sacrifices that others were not willing to. This motivation kept me going for quite some time during the summer. However, at some points I did feel like calling it quits but my friends and family were there every step of the way to encourage me to keep training.

At 6:00 AM, two days before the semester started, I found myself and 22 other potential scholarship candidates on the grassy mall of the UA campus stretching in preparation for the APFT. This APFT would determine if we would become contracted UA Army ROTC cadets. I was nervous but I was confident in my training. I ended up scoring a 298 out of 300 possible points. A stellar performance by Army standards (anything above 270 is viewed as exceeding the standard). 20 out of the original 22 made the cut. These 20 individuals and I became the corps of the Military Science First-Year Class or MSI class. These would be the individual's I would have to work with on a daily basis to accomplish whatever mission we were tasked with. They were my new team.

Lessons learned:

1. Self-motivation is great, but having a solid support team behind you really helps.

Chapter 4

Army ROTC...What is it?

Basically, the way Army ROTC works is that if you are a four-year scholarship winner you have the option of receiving compensation for full tuition, fees, and books-which I took since I was an out-of-state student-or having one lump sum of cash paid out to you to cover room and board. Additionally, as a cadet you are paid a monthly stipend that increases as you move through the program to help with living expenses.

As a cadet in the UA Army ROTC I was expected to attend Physical Training or PT workouts every Monday, Wednesday, and Friday from 6:00AM to 7:00AM, a once per week two hour long intro to the Army class, and a two hour cadet-run lab in which the concepts that were taught in class were applied in a practical exercise that the entire ROTC program or battalion participated in. At the end of each semester there was a cadet-led culminating Field Training Exercise or FTX that took place at Fort Huachuca, AZ. During the FTX all of the skills and concepts that were learned in the classroom were put to the test during this three day event. On top of all of this I was expected to be enrolled as a full-time student on track to graduate with my chosen degree (which can be any degree) in four years. For the most part, as an ROTC cadet you spend about ten hours a week playing and acting like an Army soldier and the rest of your time living a normal life. However, in uniform or not, all cadets are expected to live by the 7 Core Army Values of Loyalty, Duty, Responsibility, Selfless-Service, Honesty, Integrity, and Personal Courage.

In the once per week class, the cohort of freshman cadets both contracted and another group of individuals seeking a contract were introduced to a curriculum that included: basic Army culture, such as customs and courtesies, small unit tactics, basic first-aid training, and weapons familiarization.

Each year, as one moves up in ROTC the curriculum gets progressively more intense, the time one spends doing ROTC related activities increases, and one's duties and responsibilities to the battalion also increases.

One's freshman and sophomore years are fairly relaxed. Your main responsibilities include: building your academic GPA, keeping physically fit, paying attention in ROTC class, and being a good follower to the upper classman who are the ones with the responsibility of planning, executing, and overseeing most of the battalion's activities. Everything one is exposed to as a freshman and sophomore or MSI and MSII is in preparation for the all-important MSIII year or junior year. During this year the MSIII class takes command of all of the MSI and MSII classes which are organized into a typical Army unit. The entire corps of cadets to include all upper and underclassman is called the battalion. Within the battalion is the battalion staff or seniors (MSIV) who plan all of the ROTC events. From there, is a company. A company includes about 200 MSI, II, and III's and is led by an MSIII. Within the company are three platoons of about 40-60 cadets. Within each platoon are four squads with about 8-12 cadets and each squad is led by an MSIII. Finally, within each squad are two teams of about 3-5 cadets who are led by either a senior MSII or a very motivated and skilled MSI. Each MSIII rotates through each position and is evaluated by an MSIV (using the Leadership Development Process or LDP criterion) to determine how well that MSIII performed their duties and led their assigned cadets. These evaluations take place throughout the semester and are used as a gauge to determine the leadership ability of an MSIII. Throughout the year the MSIII's are constantly preparing for the Army's commissioning school for cadets; The Leadership Development Assessment Course at Fort Lewis Washington, better known as LDAC. LDAC is basically every Army ROTC cadet's final exam. It is a 28 day-long school that all MSIII cadets attend the summer between their junior and senior year. At LDAC, cadets from all around the country are organized into similar units like the ones described above and forced to work together under harsh circumstances to complete various missions that are all centered around a common training scenario.

The evaluations each MSIII receives at LDAC, along with the evaluations received during the school year, the cadet's cumulative GPA, and APFT score are entered into a very complex algorithm that produces the cadet's ranking among all the other MSIII's in the entire country. This list of ranked cadets makes up that year's National Order of Merit List or OML. The better one's ranking, the higher they are on the OML. The OML is what is used to determine which cadets will be selected for Active Duty and which will be selected for National Guard or Army Reserve Duty. Additionally, the OML is used to determine the branches or jobs of the cadets who were selected for active duty. The higher on the OML a cadet is the greater chance that the cadet will receive their preferred Army job or branch of choice.

By the time the National OML comes out, MSIII's are now MSIV's and make up the new battalion staff within the program and are also in the process of completing their last year of college. As battalion staff, MSIV's are responsible for planning, from a big picture stand point, all of the operations and ROTC related activities within the battalion for the MSIII's to carryout.

Their curriculum includes classes about basic officership, expectations of officers, and duties of platoon leaders. Upon graduation the MSIV's are commissioned as Second Lieutenants and their Army career begins.

Lessons learned:

1. Pay attention when you're an MSI and MSII because come MSIII year you will be expected to know everything.

Chapter 5

My first year

Before coming to college I was unsure about what I wanted to study-there are so many choices-so I didn't choose a major my first semester. I decided I was going to just focus on the basic classes that nearly all majors require, This is a common strategy for typical freshmen in college. The idea is that you take a few basic classes while to try and find out what interests you. After you have identified what you would like to study you then go through the process of declaring that specific major.-However, I was not typical, and I did not realize that waiting to select a major would come back to bite me a few years down the road.

As school began, I discovered Freshman Freedom! I was no longer pressed by my parents to do household chores, I could eat in front of the TV, and stay out as late as I wanted. I lived off-campus because I was admitted to the UofA late. It was a bit isolating so I didn't have many friends the first couple of weeks of school. I knew a few guys that lived in my complex and there were always the other 22 cadets in my MSI class, but I thought most of them were really not my type. I decided to pledge a fraternity so I could experience the true college life. Initially, I was very excited about the fraternity. As I bonded with the guys in my pledge class and played slave to the active members I began to feel the type of comradery that had long been absent since my final football season ended. However, the closer I got with the individuals in the fraternity the less interested I became in ROTC. During my time as a pledge I began to distance myself from ROTC and began developing a poor attitude toward the program. I was much more interested in partying, running from the cops, and hitting on girls with my fraternity brothers than I was learning how to field dress a fake gunshot wound. It was a bit difficult to do fraternity events and ROTC. Plus I had to learn how to balance party nights and early morning PT, which I was unsuccessful at.

It didn't help that along with getting drunk every night with my fraternity brothers, I also befriended another group of friends who were even wilder than the guys in the fraternity. We partied hard, that is for sure! It was a blast and as the semester progressed I found myself wishing I did not have ROTC duties so that I could stay out all night, any night. This group of friends greatly enhanced my partying habits and social life but reduced my interest in ROTC even more so than before. Now every time I had to wake-up early or do something on a Saturday for ROTC I just thought about the fact that I wasn't out having a good time with my friends. By the end of the first semester, I was beginning to believe that ROTC was not for me.

When I went back home to New Mexico for a long weekend, I planned on telling my mom that I was not happy with ROTC and that I did not see myself continuing with the program. I knew my mom would be opposed to me foregoing a full-ride scholarship, so before I had the sit-down talk with her I had put together several courses of action that I thought would allow me to dis-enroll from ROTC but still remain at the UA. One morning we stopped in at the Barnes & Nobel Café. It was really the first time we had had a moment to visit. My sister wondered off. So I thought it was a good time to talk about my change of plans. I started by telling my mom just how much I loved the university. I elaborated on all the great things about the school, campus life, people, instructors, etc. My mom seemed pleased to hear that and proceeded to remind me of how fortunate I was to be able to go to UA. Oh no!! So I gently broached the topic of ROTC, stating , "I am not so sure I like the ROTC part of what I am doing." She immediately said, "Well that is okay, you do not need to do that, it is your choice." I was so relieved. I told her I would like to stay at the university though. She was very calm, she shook her head and said, " Oh Daniel, that is not possible. You are there because of the Army. If you do not do ROTC that is fine, but you will come home and go to the local university, which is very good!" I couldn't believe it! Really, me? Go back home? I said, "No way, Mom. I don't want to do that." She responded, "Honey the out of state tuition is too high and you don't even have a major!" Desperately, I suggested, " How 'bout I work and go to school part time? That way I could stay at UA? She smiled and said," Honey, you will be done in three years if you stay the course, if not you won't get your degree until you're 28 or 30 years old! That is not an option. You are at the UA because of ROTC. Don't forget that." She added, "College is only temporary, think about your life beyond that."

I thought about that a lot after I got back to school that spring. ROTC really was not that bad, and it was something I could put up with because there was no way in hell I was going back home for college. Eventually, I decided that ROTC was too easy of a gig to not keep doing it.

Lessons learned:

1. Apply for a dorm early! Live on campus your freshman year. You will meet more friends.
2. College is full of new experiences, people, and situations. Find your calling no matter what it is and run with it full speed ahead.
3. Don't let others make decisions for you. Don't let others influence you in ways that compromise your values.
4. The people closest to you know you best. Tell them how you feel, listen to them, and then pray about it.
5. Moms are really smart. Give yours a hug.

Chapter 6

My second year: I gotta new attitude

Before heading back to the UA for my second year I decided improve my attitude towards ROTC. During that summer, I contacted Major Nakamoto inquiring about attending the NMSU ROTC morning PT sessions. I felt that this would not only keep me in shape but also help develop my Army mentality by exposing me to more and more military customs and nuances. At the conclusion of the summer I made the decision to live in the ROTC quarters of Cochise Dormitory on the UA campus. (My mom had gone ahead and put down the deposit even though I wasn't sure I wanted to live on campus.) My thought process in doing this was basically trying to convince myself that, if I was more engulfed in military culture that I would learn to like this ROTC gig a lot more. I think the main reason I decided to make a conscious effort to improve my attitude toward ROTC was because of the opportunities that were available to me now that I was an MS II. I was starting to look ahead mainly because Army ROTC MSII's have priority to all summer training programs that the Army allows cadets to attend. These programs include schools like: Airborne School, Air Assault School, Mountain Warfare School, Cultural Understanding Language Proficiency Program (CULP), and the most prestigious and rigorous school in the entire Army Combat Diver Qualification Course (CDQC). When I learned that the Army would send me to one of these schools, if I was competitive enough, I knew to find a way to get myself to one of these. However, I knew the only way to be selected to attend one of these schools was to be at the top of the MSII OML, which was calculated by cumulative GPA, APFT score, and instructor discretion. Interestingly, now I really wanted something from ROTC.

My grades were good and my PT score was already excellent, but given my reputation for partying and bad mouthing ROTC I was viewed by the instructors as more of a loose cannon and liability than a prospect for summer training.

Note from ROTC Instructor Mark Tatum

Daniel Coffeen started out like every other cadet who just came to college at the University of Arizona, early in the morning at 0530 hrs checking his height and weight then walking out towards the mall to start the physical fitness test (push up, sit up and 2 Mile run). At the very outset we could see he was in shape and ready for the physical demands of being a cadet.

What I remember past that as an incoming freshman/cadet at the university is that Daniel had a way of pushing people away and isolating himself from the other cadets in the program. He was respectful and cordial to the cadre and staff, but that is where his respect and politeness stopped and his aggressiveness and attitude began with the other cadets in the program.

We as a staff didn't catch on for a while and began to see him back talk cadets and challenge others in authority. Daniel provided a great opportunity for the MSIV's and MS III's to test their leadership ability and command authority that they were given by the PMS/PMI and the Commander of cadets.

As the fall semester was wrapping up for the cadets a few of the senior cadets approached me with the question of how to handle and convince him to stop making them look weak and ineffective. I told them the best answer I had, which was to figure it out? And fix it, Before the Command found out.

During one Wednesday (Cadet Leadership Training) Daniel became very confrontational with an MSIV in a very public way (That was the straw that broke the camel's back). I called Daniel over to me and started to dig into him at the same time the Senior Military Instructor (SMI) MSG Varble also joined me in verbally correcting Daniel, and letting him know his behavior would not be tolerated or accepted not only in ROTC but in the Army as well. You can't go around questioning everything and challenging everyone just because you can, and bully people because you can.

You have to understand that Daniel is 1.Very intelligent 2. Physically gifted 3. Has God given leadership ability 4.Charismatic 5.Very focused and lastly bull headed, and he comes from a hard working family who instilled their values and passion for life.

When the spring semester started Daniel started drifting away from the other cadets and started hanging around other students at the University, so I thought. As usual I started inquiring about Daniel with other cadets in the program about his change of behavior. I asked Daniel about his lack of focus and his drop in his physical fitness and overall demeanor.

Sometime during the semester I found out he pledged into a fraternity and was spending a lot of his time with them. One cadet (female) stated that those guys where assholes and drunks. At that time during a training event I ask him if he was Ok! He gave me an answer but it lacked conviction and was just to get me out his face. I thought we lost Daniel and we might have to ask him to leave the program or he was going to leave under his own volition.

But life happens sometime during the fall of 2010, he had a huge blow out with his fraternity brothers or should I say the President the fraternity in an angry tirade. Just rumored around the because of their lack of civility toward woman. After that he was distant in a different way he became focused and began showing up early and often, engaged with others and the program as a whole.

During the spring of 2011 Daniel came to me and apologized for his behavior in the past and vowed to make up for it and that his head was strait and he was focused on College and ROTC. It first manifested on the first weekend training event he was a great follower, not questioning but offering advice and guidance to other cadets.

He went on to continue his rise in the program and was selected for some very selective summer programs that would test him not only physically, but mentally also.

Ch. 7

Big Changes Ahead

I knew I had to completely restructure my lifestyle and revitalize my image among the ROTC community if I was going to make it in the program. During my MSII year, that is exactly what I did. I worked hard that year, deliberately going above and beyond what was expected of me in the ROTC program. By that spring, I was ranked number one on the MSII OML and awarded a slot to attend The Army's 8-week Special Forces Combat Diver Qualification Course in Key West, FL. Mission Accomplished! However, none of this would have been possible without a very unique person who entered my life that year.

Michael Van Liew, the oldest child from a wealthy-suburban New Jersey family. Michael was assigned to be my roommate in Cochise Dormitory. Similar to me, Michael had received a 4-year federally funded Navy ROTC scholarship, although he had elected to enroll in the Marine Corps division of the Navy program. Michael was the model cadet and student. He had never touched alcohol or drugs, never went to parties, never cursed, exercised constantly, got good grades, befriended everyone, and spent his free time reading up on Marine Corps history and tactical doctrine. All of Michael's tendencies, quite honestly made me sick. After the first few weeks of living with him and realizing that he had stayed into study every single weekend I thought there had to be something wrong with him. However, as time went on and we got to know each other more I realized it was me who was wrong. Michael had definitive-achievable goals and a roadmap to attain them. He wanted to serve his country as a Marine Air Ground Task Force Officer. Conversely, I had an idea and a few haphazard assumptions on how to get what I wanted. As the year went on I began to spend more time with Michael. I learned from him and he exposed me to what motivated him to serve his country. More importantly, as I spent more and more time with Michael, the desire to serve that I once had before coming to college was beginning to come back. It was a great feeling.

As the year went on Michael and I became inseparable, I ended up dropping the fraternity I had pledged and pretty much abandoned the group of non-ROTC friends who had blinded me from my desire to serve (I would eventually recover these lost relationships down the road). As a result, not only did my image and repoire with my ROTC colleagues and instructors improve but I actually began to enjoy ROTC. I began researching the history of the Army. Diligently I became a student of leadership. I found myself researching-new techniques on how to lead and how to develop winning attitudes among my subordinates and peers. What a turnaround, right?

As I look back on it now, the new attitude and mindset that I developed over the course of my MSII year really wasn't new at all. It was actually everything I had learned and done playing football in high school; by applying the strategies my coaches taught me. Same thing, only in a new setting. As my MSII or sophomore year ended I was excited about receiving my slot to CDQC and was primed and ready to tackle one of the biggest challenges of my life. However, I was saddened at the fact that Michael would not be coming back to the UA. He had decided to transfer his scholarship to The Citadel in South Carolina in order to be closer to his family. He had made such a profound impact on my life. I will be forever grateful.

Postcard from CDQC

So here I was only 19 years old getting ready to fly off to Key West, Fl for the United Sates Army Combat Diver Qualification Course; the most challenging and intense school in the Army with a higher attrition rate than any other school in the military. Being one of only a handful of cadets in a training school created for Special Forces Green Berets was an honor but overwhelmingly intimidating. At the time I was just excited about fulfilling all of the requirements in order to be selected to attend the school. I had a general idea of what to expect during the 8 week school, however, little did I know what I had worked so hard to get myself into.

I took a trip home for a visit before I left to Key West. My family and friends were very proud of me for getting into this school, even though they knew it would be tough for me to survive the entire 8 weeks. My Uncle Mike was one of my biggest supporters. He gave me his very expensive TAG Heuer diving watch one afternoon. He cut a deal with me. If I completed CDQC and became Combat Diver Qualified he would allow me to keep the watch. Both of us were so confident that I was going to pass that we didn't even bother entertaining the other aspect of the deal.

Dive school was an amazing experience. Upon arrival my first roommate was a swimmer from West Point named Ayman Andrews. He was a great guy with a colorful personality to say the least, but the kid had a mouth on him and he became notorious for "mouthing off" to the dive supervisors. As a result, we all paid for it with copious amounts of flutter kicks. I actually didn't mind the punishment because I really liked Ayman. I admired his confidence and his no BS attitude. However, he did snore incredibly loud which irritated me more than anything. I remember thinking it was going be a long 8 weeks.

The PT we conducted every morning was incredibly challenging. The runs were led by a former marathoner and were conducted at an incredible pace. I was a good runner but I was in no way, shape or form prepared for this type of running. Plus this school taking place in the heart of summer with Florida humidity didn't help things much either. However, after the first week, I got a tip from one of the other individuals in the school, SFC Agrell, a 27 year old Special Forces Combat Engineer. He advised me to save my energy but make it look like I was working hard during PT. This would show that I was putting forth the necessary effort but secretly it would allow me to save my energy for the extremely important pool training that we conducted during the day. Initially I had never thought about this and I was a bit hesitant to try it out, but I was desperate. Quite honestly, morning PT was kicking my ass and I was paying for it in the pool I am the kind of person who pushes himself no matter the circumstances. However, this individual conveyed to me that CDQC had nothing to do with impressing the instructors, it was all about survival. I didn't like the thought of "faking the funk" but I had to survive.

Early on in the school we started with a 1000 meter swim and gradually increased each day to 3000 meters. The first surface swim was where, based on ability, we were paired with our dive buddy and new roommate. From that day forward we conducted surface swims every afternoon in full ACU's (Army Combat Uniform), BCD (Buoyancy Control Device), fins, and mask. Fighting ocean currents and avoiding snapping turtles is no walk in the park. It was rigorous and exhausting.

After that initial surface swim I was paired with CPT. Luke Self of 10th Special Forces Group out of Fort Carson, Co my new roommate. CPT Self was extremely motivated and incredibly spiritual. At some points during the training he was kind of a downer, mainly because I think he missed his wife, I could just tell. We were dive team 15 ranked out of 30, which indicated our ability level, pretty much middle of the pack. I was okay with our standing because I wanted to keep myself under the radar as much as possible. Being one of the only cadets in a school created for Special Forces Green Berets who have been through some of the most rigorous training the Army has to offer and who have probably killed men with their bare hands, is intimidating as hell! Let's just say it is a tad bit difficult, as a cadet to gain the respect of such battle-hardened veterans. How do you gain any credibility when the most "Hooah" (Army lingo for Bad Ass) thing you have ever done involved a paintball gun and taped up tennis balls? Well, you don't.

When we weren't getting our ass kicked in the pool or fighting ridiculous ocean currents we were in the classroom trying to stay awake and learn. In the classroom we learned about dive physics, diving physiology, dive injuries, decompression charts, Boyle's Law, Newton's Law, and all those physics legends whose names I can't remember, I had never been exposed to any of this information and was not expecting this academic dimension at all. As a result, while everyone else was sleeping at night I was up hitting the books for some late night studying before the exams.

The food served in the chow hall was by far the best food I had ever eaten on a military installation. We were instructed to eat a lot of calories to keep our energy levels high, but not so much that we would feel sick during training (I learned the hard way, but finally found the right balance).

Throughout the 8-week long course I was lucky enough to make it through all of the hard tasks: the APFT, the 5 mile run in under 40 minutes, all of the pool events, and all of the classroom exams. I was doing well and it seemed that everybody, including the Green Berets liked me. The instructors liked me too, they even gave me a nickname, McLovin. Self-explanatory. So much for staying under the radar.

During a training event which required us to ditch and don the set of the twin 80 cubic foot breathing apparatuses we wore underwater, I committed a safety violation that resulted in my early release from CDQC. I blame this on the fact that I was overly prepared for the ditch and don test. I had practiced on land the night before and completed five practice rounds in the water (three regular and two with a blacked out mask) before the actual graded test. All of the practice rounds went perfectly and I was feeling confident for the exam. Then we were pulled from the pool, read the terms of the test, and called out individually to be tested. I was one of the last ones called and had to use the bathroom bad! However, I just wanted to get done with the test so that I could begin studying for the physics exam we had coming up that afternoon. I got in the pool, ditched all of my gear properly but messed up the Free Swimming Assent (FSA) which got me sent to retraining to be retested. My instructor at the original test, MSG Reed, was a real jerk to me. He said some things to me that really had me feeling pretty worthless for screwing up such a simple task. I was pissed and dishearten that I failed. The retraining I was sent to went well, but I was still feeling sorry for myself (this is where I learned that you must have a short memory). Then we went to lunch. After lunch the re-testers had to go back to the pool immediately after eating. As the re-testers went back to the pool everyone else was able to go back to their rooms and prepare for the upcoming physics exam. At the pool we were given the option to either re-take the test right then or wait 24 hours and take the test the following day. Still fuming that I had failed once already and now not able to study for the exam I decided to waive the 24 hour wait period and just get the test over with. Mistake. Again, I was the last one called to take the test and still pretty pissed off. I ditched and conducted the FSA properly. Then I donned my gear and as I was doing my self-equipment check I noticed a twist in one of my shoulder straps. Since this was a timed test I began to panic, not sure if I had enough time to fix the twist. I knew if I left the twist in the strap points would be deducted from my final score and I may not pass. I elected to re-ditched all of my gear knowing that now I was really pressed for time. I got the twist out, did my safety checks again and gave the signal to be graded. The grader, SFC. Tabbert, did not swim down to me when he saw the signal. At that point I knew it was over. My initial thought after the avalanche of emotion and disappointment had buried me was that I had ran out of time. In fact, as I learned moments later upon surfacing, that I had failed to inspect my waist strap a second time after re-donning all of my equipment. I knew that was bullshit but I was done, labeled a failure, and would be sent home.

I had been prepared, I was ready. I had these safety checks down pat. I had completed more practice iterations than anyone in the entire class. However, to my own surprise I didn't protest. Surprisingly, I was immediately overcome with relief. I felt a burst of energy like I had never felt before. For a split second the only thing I could think about was my family back home and the family that I planned on having in the future. Right then and there, on that pool deck, I knew I did not want to be a combat diver or any type of combat specialist for that matter. My life had taken a new direction in a split second. All I knew was that I wanted to do three things; serve my country, make a lot of money, and raise a beautiful family. As SFC Tabbert looked at me, waiting for a reply, I smiled politely, shook his hand, and thanked him for the opportunity. I dropped all my gear on the pool deck and headed to my room to pack my things and call my mom. As I walked back to my room I reflected on the people I had met and all of the experiences I had had over the past few weeks. It had been a blast, I had learned so much from these crazy older guys who had done so much for our country. Flying home that day, I came to the realization that CDQC and this type of lifestyle was not for me.

Looking back, I never really wanted to be a combat diver in the first place. I was looking for prestige and honor. That's why I went after that goal. I decided to set my goals a little more carefully and be clearer on my motives in the future. Moreover, I was pretty sure that I didn't want a career in the Army that was directly combat related. After much thought I believed my leadership skills would be best utilized in the medical field as a Medical Services Officer. That was my new goal.

I realized there was a larger reason that I didn't graduate from CDQC. I was physically fit, mentally capable and prepared. The reason was larger than anything that I had control over, it was just not meant to be. I realized God had bigger and better plans for me, a new journey, and I was excited to see where they would take me. However, I did know my first stop on my new journey...home.

Lessons learned:

1. If there is something you want, declare it, and make it the most important thing in your life.
2. You never know what people have to offer you or how others can impact your state of mind.
3. Enjoy the opportunities and experiences you get. Keep a journal and keep track of those around you.
4. Accept your successes and your failures and learn from them. Think about them and take meaning away from each experience in order to help yourself and other down the road.
5. Understand that everything happens for a reason and in the end, it will all work out, maybe not as you had originally planned, but it will all work out.
6. Understand that an unmet goal is a learning experience and an opportunity to change your course.
7. Start looking ahead – beyond today, this week, this month, this year. Decide what you want, declare it, and make it the most important thing in your life.
8. Have attainable and achievable goals complete with a road map from start to finish.
9. Seek out and get to know those that are serious about what interests you. You never know what people have to offer you or how others can impact your state of mind.

Chapter 8

My Third Year

As the summer between my MSII and MSIII year passed I reflected a lot on the changes I had made during my MSII year and the life changing experiences I had at CDQC. Knowing that my most important year of ROTC was fast approaching I decided to take my motivation, desire to serve, and academic and PT focus to an all-time high. For the fall semester I tacked on 23 credits of rigorous course work in order to increase my GPA; Even though I wasn't even of age I stopped drinking all types of alcohol; skipped out on nearly all late night hangouts with friends; unplugged my TV; and substituted my casual reading of Sports Illustrated for Army Field Manuals and military readiness books. At the beginning of the semester I also, unexpectedly, began dating a girl. At the time she seemed to me as a more of a distraction than anything else but I was too nice of a person to dump her. However, as I look back on it I believe that she really helped keep me sane during the fall semester. Moreover, she was a year older than me and also in ROTC. So not only was she a person who supported me and cared about me but she was also full of knowledge and helpful hints about LDAC, which I was scheduled to attend the upcoming summer.

On the first day of school of my MSIII year, I thought it would be a good idea to give a speech to the rest of my MSIII classmates. I wanted to express to them my goals for that year and introduce them to my roadmap of attaining those goals. I touched on teamwork, leading by example, and developing relationships with others. In doing this I unintentionally distinguished myself as the leader of the MSIII class. To my advantage, assuming this role allowed me to further develop the already revived relationship with my instructors and helped me gain the trust of my fellow MSIII's.

Throughout my MSIII year, my garrison evaluations, increasing GPA, and nearly untouchable APFT score landed me once again at the top of the MSIII OML at the end of the semester. As a reward I was presented with the opportunity to travel to the United States Military Academy at West Point for the National Conference on Ethics in America. However, as I was busy with school, travel, working out, and trying to be the best I could be at ROTC I developed a very selfish attitude. I felt that since I was working so hard to attain my academic and ROTC related goals, my fellow MSIII's should have been working just as hard and been just as motivated as I was. Although most of them were motivated and willing to do whatever it took to improve their position on the OML I was blind to this. In passing I would sometimes scoff at them for what I thought were poor efforts on their part. I viewed myself as superior to them. In short, having this particular view of superiority, I burned a lot of bridges and damaged a lot of friendships that I should not have and wish I had never done. However, none of this was made as clear to me as when we were given a peer evaluation assignment.

In the peer evaluation assignment every cadet had to write at a minimum of two improves and two sustains for every one of their classmate's leadership ability; based on anything character or ROTC related that they had observed over the fall semester. For me, most of the sustains addressed my high level of motivation and willingness to go the extra mile. I had anticipated most of these. However, the improves, which were all shockingly similar across the board, had to do with my bad habit of exploiting peoples faults, correcting and embarrassing people in front of others, and my inability to be a follower without forcing my views upon the group. At this point in time I was literally unaware of these things, so seeing these anonymous evaluations really opened my eyes to the type of leader and person I was becoming. I knew in the back of my mind that this was not the person I was and that I needed to do some restructuring of my interpersonal skills and leadership style for two reasons. To rebuild some of the relationships I had damaged and to ensure that I didn't come off as arrogant or viewing myself as superior when I got to LDAC.

Much of the spring semester of my MSIII year was similar to the fall semester, minus the girlfriend. I had a fully loaded 20 credit hour school schedule and was absolutely bogged down with ROTC related activities. At this point I was very focused on refining my skills for LDAC. I would conduct supplemental land navigation and orienteering practice at a local park in Tucson in order to keep my navigating and map reading skills sharp. Also, several times a week I would convince one of the MSIV seniors to do a tactical operations order drill with me. This consisted of them quickly reading me a pre-drafted enemy situation; me developing a plan to address the enemy situation; and finally briefing the plan I had created back to them all within 25 minutes. Most importantly, I did well in school that semester. I ended the semester with a 4.0 GPA. I was now primed and ready for the biggest test of my ROTC career, LDAC.

Lessons learned:

1. Leading by example is a good way to get people to follow you.

2. Hard work only brings more hard work and in time people will notice and you will be rewarded for your efforts.
3. Personal development is important but only when it does not negatively affect those around you.

Chapter 9

LDAC

Since I was still a little bit behind on my credits I had elected to attend the first session of summer school, so I could graduate on time. That being the case I was slotted to go to Fort Lewis, WA for LDAC from July 2nd to July 30th, the 11th regiment. During the previous-spring semester our ROTC instructors had given us all the hints and tips that could contribute to our success at LDAC. In an effort to excel at LDAC I began to listen very closely to my instructors, I began to understand that they really were there to help us succeed. I studied and went over every point from land navigation to tactics, with the most emphasis focused on interacting with people, being open to new ideas and keeping a positive attitude. Going into LDAC I decided I was going to do just that.

Some cadets will tell you that one must be focused and treat LDAC like the most important event in your life, however, I decided I was going to take a more relaxed approach and treat LDAC, like it was a summer camp experience. You know the ones you see on TV where everyone sleeps in cabins, plays sports during the day, and tell ghost stories at night. I wanted to keep the environment light and relaxed. ROTC has a tendency to be very serious and it can be a real buzzkill even when the situation should be fun. I wanted to make as many friends as I could. I was starting to realize that relationships were important. I wanted to make sure that every morning when I woke up, no matter how early it was or how tired and cold I was, I was going to have a smile on my face. I wanted to be the person that the individuals in my assigned platoon could turn to if they needed some encouragement. So that is what I did.

Additionally, I told myself that I was going to focus on recognizing others when they did something correctly and less on correcting an individual if they did something wrong. I also decided that I would make it a point to learn everyone in my platoon's first name, and to call them by that name. It may seem odd but it is the nature of the Army to call everyone by their last name. It's not that I have anything against last names, I just feel that when somebody knows and addresses me by my first name that they took the time to learn and remember something about me and are not just reading the name that is printed on the left side of my uniform.

Throughout the different testing, training events, and leadership rotations that my platoon endured during LDAC, I worked on building solid relationships with nearly every cadet, something I had failed to do back at school in my freshman and sophomore year. I took interest in their personal lives and made sure that they knew who they should come to if they needed assistance with a task or advice on how to complete a given task. I also made myself available to be utilized for petty jobs like cleaning the bathrooms or taking out the garbage and did so with a smile on my face. The relationships that I had built with these individuals paid off when it was my turn to be in charge. Because I had established good relationships with my platoon I had their support at all times. They knew that I had been willing to help them succeed and were excited about returning the favor. Probably the most important lesson I learned while I was at LDAC was that if you take care of your people, they will in turn, take care of you. I learned that small acts of kindness may seem to go unnoticed sometimes, but in the end the kindness that you show always returns itself back to you.

The relationships I built with my fellow cadets are what contributed to my success at LDAC. By the time graduation day came I had forty new best friends and had earned the following awards: Top Male APFT Award with a score of 384; The Recondo Award for the best all-around performance at Warrior Forge, achieving among the highest scores in all tasks to include the Army Physical Fitness Test, all Confidence and Assault Courses, Land navigation, Individual Tactics Training, Marksmanship, and Situational Training Exercise Leadership; The Distinguished Honor Graduate of 11th regiment by the regimental cadre, and voted the number one cadet of forty-one in my platoon, and fourth overall out of all the cadets that attended LDAC during the summer of 2012-around five thousand cadets-. Looking back I think it was 10% hard work, 0% talent, 10% physical training, and 80% attitude that allowed me to do so well at LDAC.

At this point, the end was near and I was missing home. After only short letters back and forth to my sister and mom, I was really excited and anxious about going home. However, moments before graduation I received one last award, or opportunity rather. Because of my achievements at LDAC the regimental cadre presented me with the opportunity to continue my training by participating in Cadet Command's four-week Cadet Troop Leading Time (CTLT) in Hohenfels, Germany. After this news was delivered to me, I was torn between going home and reconnecting with my family and friends or-experiencing a part of the world I had always dreamed of visiting. After consulting some of my new friends and several quick prayers I elected to go to Germany. However, there was one little problem. All I had to my name was two pairs of Army uniforms, a tooth brush, underwear, and socks. I had no money, no cell phone, no idea where in Germany I was going, when I would be back, and oh yeah, I couldn't speak a lick of German. This was going to be an adventure!

Since I elected to go to Germany I was unable to attend the graduation ceremony at the conclusion of LDAC where I was to receive the awards I had earned. So instead, the regimental cadre presented me with the awards, which included; several coins, plaques, and a really cool saber during the graduation rehearsal the day prior. After the rehearsal I received some great news. I learned that my friend and classmate from the UofA, Tyler Sams, who was from 12th Regiment would be accompanying me on my trip to Germany. Lucky for him and for me too, Tyler had earned his CTLT slot before leaving for LDAC so he had a whole suit case full of civilian clothes, a cell phone, an Ipad, and a whole lot of other goodies that I would be borrowing from him once we got to Germany.

After the 18 hour flight and an outlandish performance from the 27 infants (seriously, 27 babies, crying, the whole time on our flight!) in the plane's cabin from Washington to Ramstien Air Force Base in Germany, Tyler and I still had an eight hour bus ride to Hohenfels, Germany. Once we finally arrived on post I learned that I would be taking command of third platoon Charlie Company (Tyler had second platoon) of the 1st of the 4th Infantry Regiment at the Joint Military Readiness Center (JMRC). JMRC is basically the final stop for select U.S. and NATO units to conduct training before deploying into theater. Our daily duties consisted of leading PT and facilitating tactical training for our platoons along with our counterparts of the 1st of the 124th National Guard Infantry regiment in order to help prepare Republic of Georgian soldiers for future deployments to Afghanistan. During my time in Germany I learned a lot about how a real Army unit functions. Now seriously, think about this just a year earlier I was a punk ass sophomore at the UofA thinking I was too good for all of this and now I had this amazing experience to build my leadership skills and learn what it was to be a real soldier – I was humbled and I was grateful.

Additionally, I was exposed to something's that are common among the combat arms branches (infantry, armor, air defense artillery, field artillery, and aviation) of the Army that pushed me further away from ever wanting to be an Infantry, Armor, or any other type of combat arms officer. I'm talking about the constant pressure placed on individuals to be as masculine and malicious towards others, especially those who are weaker or of lesser rank, as possible. Some of the instances I am referring to dealt with exploiting other soldier's weaknesses, physical flaws, and lack of intelligence. This significantly decreased moral among the soldiers. When I asked some of the other officers and NCO's in the company about this, they all conveyed to me that consistent competition and the desire to be right and to crush those who are wrong is a common theme for the infantry. This did not sit well with me especially looking back at how I treated some of my friends back at school and how I had reversed that when I went to LDAC. I knew for a fact that I did not want to engulf myself in such a negative environment in the future. However, instead of having a negative attitude towards this type of Army culture I decided to embrace it and look for subtle ways to pick those up and inspire those who had been put down. After experiencing this I was certain that I wanted to be a Medical Services Officer.

On a lighter note, I had a great time touring and partying around Germany and the surrounding areas. Whenever we were not working, Tyler and I would hop on train and head to one of the various German towns. During the day we would enjoy the local food, shopping, and entertainment. However, when the sun went down is when we got really crazy. Conventional wisdom is that Germans like to drink, boy isn't that the truth. Let's just say Tyler and I drank our fair share of German beer and hugged an equal amount of public toilets.

Germany was a great experience, not only was I responsible for real soldiers conducting live Army operations I filled the platoon leader position almost the entire time I was there. I was exposed to many different people, leadership styles, and personalities that helped refine my own personal leadership style. Aside from all of the Army stuff I got to do I was able to experience European culture and create lasting memories with one of my best friends.

Lessons learned:

1. Take care of your people and they will take care of you.
2. Kindness, when given, always comes back to you.
3. Never pass up an opportunity to experience new things, especially travel.
4. Even in an unpleasant situation, one can still have a positive influence.

Chapter 9

My fourth year

After Tyler and I endured another 18 plus hours of screaming infants on our return trip from Germany, we landed back in Tucson ready for a break from all this fast paced Army stuff. However, a break was the last thing we were about to get because by the time we got back to the Tucson, school had already been in session for two weeks. So not only were we both completely burnt out and jet lagged, but we were two weeks behind in our studies. Great! So basically, I spent the entire first semester bragging about my experiences in Germany, catching up in school and trying maintain my GPA.

About mid-way through my first semester of my Senior or MSIV year the highly anticipated National OML came out. All of my classmates and I were sweaty palms nervous as then Major Ben Walters our Professor of Military Science and Battalion Commander called us each in to his office individually. When it was my turn to enter his office I was less nervous as others to find out my job in the Army would be for the next four years. I was confident that all my hard work that I had put in over the last two years had paid off. When he told me that I would be a Medical Services Officer in the Active Duty component of the Army, I knew the hard work had paid off and I was ecstatic! I was over-come with emotions and happy as hell that I didn't have to try and find a civilian job after graduation. As humble as I would like to be, I do have to brag about my national standing among all of the commissioning class of 2013. I was ranked 113 out of 5,600 cadets. After I finally figured out that this entire military experience was a gift handed to me on a silver platter (two years earlier) I worked my ass off to take full advantage of it with the hopes of writing my own ticket, and I did.

When the second semester of MSIV year rolled around (my last semester of college) I was tasked as being the Chief Operations Officer or the S3 for the Battalion. This meant that I was in charge of every single operation or ROTC related activity that would be conducted over the remainder of the year. This was a large responsibility that very few individuals are capable of handling. However, since I had taken such heavy course loads during my MSIII year, I had a fairly open schedule, allowing me more time to devote to ROTC. Besides, being the Battalion S3 is literally the best position for a soon to be Second Lieutenant to have. This is because the S3 must be an expert on military style writing, be able to delegate tasks to subordinates, and also hold individuals responsible for meeting deadlines and producing good quality work.

So really, everything was coming together far better than I could have ever planned. I finally had the right attitude. In my spare time I continued to learn as much as possible about leadership and expose myself to as much Army culture as possible. I began to reach out to various officers in the Tucson area to gain insight on military lifestyle and officership. I collaborated with several Medical Service Officers who helped me understand and navigate the Medical Service Corps.

Additionally, I was able to begin rebuilding the relationships with my classmates that I had previously damaged or neglected. After ROTC events I began organizing MSIV-only happy hours at the bars near the university. It was during this last semester that the MSIV class began spending more and more time together. We would spend hours reliving our experiences at LDAC, talking about our dream cars, and looking forward to how awesome life was going to be once we all started making money. During this time all 20 or so MSIVs grew closer together, we became one another's best friends. I think it is because we were all so relieved that we were almost done with school and so close to graduating, commissioning, and starting our lives. During that last semester I built some of the best relationships I will ever have. By far this was my memorable and enjoyable time during college.

Lessons learned:

1. Find professionals in your field and ask them questions and for their opinion on what steps you should take
2. Creating and maintaining relationships with successful and determined people who have similar values as you is very beneficial.
3. Become the glue for the team no matter what team it is. Find commonalities among its members and celebrate those to create unity. Bottom line, take care of your people and they will take care of you.
4. Never pass up an opportunity to experience new things, especially travel.
5. Even in an unpleasant situation, one can still have a positive influence.

Chapter 10

Commissioning

May 10th, commissioning day could not have come any slower. It was a beautiful ceremony on a more than sunny day in Tucson, AZ. Thank God we were inside. I and eighteen others were clean cut and freshly shaven in our Army Service Uniforms. After the greeting and the invocation, conducted by yours truly, one by one each one of my classmates approached the stage received the Oath of Office and their first salute and returned to their seat as a newly commissioned Second Lieutenant. When it was finally my turn, I was nearly breathless. As I walked down the aisle to meet Retired Navy Captain and my best friend's Dad Tom Hutchinson, my mother and grandfather, and my very good friend Michael Nakamoto I'm certain I was overcome with emotion because I'm pretty sure my hangover had subsided by then. As I approached them on stage I locked eyes with my mother and recognized the look she had on her face. I had seen it almost four years ago to the day when I was approaching a different stage at the Senior Awards Ceremony in my high school gymnasium. After I was introduced to the audience, Tom read me the Oath of Office, my mother and grandfather pinned my rank on, and Michael rendered me my first salute. The second I turned to walk off that stage I knew I had accomplished something that not many individuals can. Really for the first time I could say I was truly proud of my profession and who I was as a person. I finally felt like I could begin to give back to my country. I had wanted to serve since I was in the third grade and now it was time to do just that.

Lessons Learned:

1. Stay true to what you want in life. If you want to serve, then serve. Don't let the process negatively affect the outcome you want.

Epilogue

Upon commissioning I received orders to Medical Services Basic Officer Leaders Course (BOLC) in San Antonio, TX where I would learn everything I need to know about being a Medical Services Officer. With those orders, came the duty station where I would be working for the next three to four years. I was quite excited when I heard the news that I would be going to Schofield Barracks on the beautiful Island of Oahu, HI. However before I could begin either of these adventures I had received some fortunate luck. I was asked to begin my career a few months earlier than most of my peers by attending LDAC again. However, instead of being a cadet I would now be on the other side of the spectrum as an instructor. When I first arrived back at LDAC I was notified that I would be the Officer in Charge (OIC) of Patrolling. This was a huge responsibility. I would be held accountable for ensuring that the patrolling lanes conducted by the cadets ran smoothly without any error. I would be in charge of a group of actual enlisted soldiers who were stationed at Fort Lewis who would be supplementing the patrolling lanes as the mock enemy. During my time as a Patrolling OIC I learned a lot about the Army way of life. I learned how to act around junior and senior enlisted men as well as Company and Field Grade Officers. I am thankful that I had the opportunity to start my Army career early and it's not because the money was good. Because the money was really good! It is because it gave me a head start and a preview to what the real Army is like. It gave me the chance to make mistakes and learn from them without any repercussions. Similar to the first time, LDAC the second time around was a great experience. I made many friends and learned a several valuable lessons that I will carry with me the rest of my career.

Lessons Learned

1. Get your rank sewn on your hat.
2. If you get a citation from the MP's on Post, tell your commander.